Self-Made

Real Australian Business Stories

Busybird Publishing
PO Box 855 Eltham
Victoria Australia 3095
www.busybird.com.au

First published by Busybird Publishing 2014

ISBN 978-0-9924874-3-0

Editor: Les Zigomanis

Typeset in Palatino 12pt

Printed and bound by McPherson's Printing Group

*This book is dedicated to those
brave enough to live their dreams
and take control of their life.*

Contents

Introduction

There are many people who go to work every day and count the hours to knock off, then count the days until the weekend. If you aren't happy in your job then those forty or so hours every week will feel like drudgery. This can be especially frustrating if you are good at your job but don't get the credit or pay that you deserve.

Imagine going to work every day, loving what you do. Imagine having the freedom to do *what* you want, *when* you want. This is possible if you have your own business, although admittedly running your own business can be fraught with danger.

Being good at something doesn't mean that you will be good at running a business. Proof of this lies in the numbers from the Australian Bureau of Statistics that 60% of small businesses fail in their first three years. The main reasons for this are lack of experience, poor location, poor financial control, ineffective management, and inadequate cash flow.

You can learn to run a business successfully if you seek out the right advice. This is difficult if you don't know what you need or where to start. You don't know the questions to ask if you don't know what they are! This book is designed to give any would-be business owner a kick-start to running a business.

Eight professionals who work in small business share their stories – the brilliant, the good and the ugly – in the hope that you might be saved years of money, hard work and unnecessary mistakes.

These people have made their own way but have had to struggle with many obstacles along the way.

These stories will help you avoid the pitfalls and equip you on the road to freedom.

Have a Crack

Justin Fankhauser

Justin is the co-owner (along with Brad Haber) and director of Toplock Locksmiths. He's 39, married to Jo, and has two kids, Lily and Jensen.

Before becoming a locksmith, I had over 20 different jobs. Amongst them, I'd been a salesman, council worker, barman, and storeman. I am also a qualified pastry cook/baker. I'm a big advocate for having a go in life and in business. Find something you love and you will never work a day in your life.

I wasn't very good at school, especially with spelling and mathematics, but one thing I was good at was working with my hands. I didn't really like school, so two days after my 15th birthday I left to complete an apprenticeship as a baker/pastry cook. I'd only completed a Year 8 education, so to say I was a puppy is an understatement.

I worked really hard to complete this apprenticeship and by the age of 19 I was qualified, but I knew this was not something I wanted to do forever. I worked and ran a few bakeries around Melbourne, then at the age of 21 I decided to travel, so I packed my bags and headed to the UK, travelling around Europe. I found this to be a great learning time in my life. It opened my eyes up to the world and life. I worked in bars, supermarkets and restaurants, but travelling and meeting different people was the biggest pleasure.

At the age of 22, I met Jo, the woman who would become my wife. One year after meeting her, we were married. We decided to come back to Australia to live, work and start a family. This is where things changed for me in my career.

It was the 90s and the country was going through a recession. Work was hard to find. I continued to work as a pastry cook, but this was something I was not

2

enjoying. I had a go at selling advertising but didn't like selling something that you couldn't touch and feel. It was hard to try to change my career because of my education. Every job I went for, they would ask, 'Did you complete your HSC [Year 12]?' It was hard not to think that, because of my lower form of education, I would never be able to do something different. My wife ended up getting me a job at her work as a storeman/driver.

Around this time I got burgled. I said to myself, 'I thought locks kept the bad guys out'. About six months after this I locked myself out of my house. It was a Friday night. The pay working as a storeman/driver wasn't great, so I supplemented my income by working all night in my mate's bakery for $120, which I thought was great money. I rang a locksmith who opened my door in about a minute and charged me $120. Wow, that's great money for the amount of time he took to open my door. I talked to him about his job and he told me he loved what he does. Wow, this is what I want, I thought. Something where I meet people, work for myself and love what I do.

The locksmith suggested I go back to night school and learn to become a locksmith. The thought of this really excited me so, for the next two years, two nights a week, I went to night school at NMIT in Heidelberg. I learnt my new trade – locksmithing.

This was a tough time for me. I worked Monday to Friday as a driver/storeman, and worked part time in my mate's bakery Monday and Wednesday nights. My classes were Tuesday and Thursday nights, and to top that all off, I worked all night Friday night at the bakery. I did this for two years. It nearly killed me, but I knew it would be all worth it someday. After completing my course, I worked in a few locksmith shops around Melbourne, honing my skills.

I finally knew what I wanted to do, so it was now time to have a go at doing it for myself. I saved up $5K and bought a station wagon. Toplock Locksmiths was now born. The day I resigned from work, I came home and cried on the couch thinking, What have I done? I'm not educated, I've never done anything for myself before.

It was a tough time for me, but I kept telling myself I could do anything if I put my mind to it. So with that I got myself together. Just keep punching; I'll do it, I thought. The next day, I got up early and decided to drop my business card off to as many businesses and people I could. To my surprise, by the end of the day I had booked in two jobs. I was over the moon. My new life had begun.

Toplock Locksmiths is one of the largest locksmith companies in Melbourne. We have ten staff and now complete over 100 jobs per week. We are a fully mobile service that specialises in all things security, from lockouts, supplying and fitting deadlocks and window locks, rekeying, alarms, and CCTV – just to name a few. We do domestic and commercial real estate, bodycorp work, 24 hours/7 days a week. We are located in Northcote, Victoria and have five fully-equipped vehicles on the road.

I often get asked, 'What are the main things in business you have done that has made Toplock into a successful business?' So, here we go:

Be different in business. If you find out what you love doing and want to turn it into a business, do it differently to everybody else. If you do things differently, you won't have any competitors. It amazes me how many people open a business and copy someone else's ideas in the same industry. At Toplock, I always try to be different to my opposition. For example, I do YouTube videos, I have apps, I write books about our industry, we write blogs, I do talks about the security industry and attend network meetings. We brand ourselves differently. If you look at our website you will soon understand what we do as a business to be different. Remember, people love doing business with people who don't do it like everybody else. Don't be scared to be different. I bet Richard Branson didn't.

Have fun. I know business is serious

stuff, but making it fun for you, your staff and customers always makes your business stand out. People love dealing with businesses that are professional but also love dealing with owners who like to have a laugh. Remember, we are all only human, and there is a funny side to things sometimes.

Get used to working hard. I thought when I worked for someone that I worked really hard. I soon learnt that I had it easy. In business, you will always be working, not just on the job but your staff, your books, thinking about advertising, cash flow, networking, etc. I do around 60 to 80 hours a week in my business every week, but because I love what I do it feels like I don't work at all. So if you don't want to work hard and you don't love what you do, don't start a business because it won't work. I know this sounds harsh, but it's true. I remember Lindsay Fox saying, 'The harder I work, the luckier I become.' This is so true, so remember that you must work hard to climb the mountain to see the view. I work extremely hard within my business and, like Lindsay, the harder I've worked the luckier I've become, believe me.

Lastly, and most importantly, have a go and don't give up. Every day, in business and in life, I come across things that scare me, but the one thing I always do is have a go and I never give up. Most people in business and in life always take the easy option. In business, I always have a go. Even if it doesn't work out, at least you had a crack. I'm not saying do something that will send you broke, but when you think something's too hard, don't walk away. Give it a shot and you may be surprised.

One day I walked into an agent to give the details of my business in the hope of getting work. The property manager was rude to me. Maybe she was having a bad day. I walked out with my tail between my legs and I thought to myself, This is too hard, but the next day I went straight back in, even though I didn't want to. I asked for the same property manager and said, 'Please give me a go.' I promised her I wouldn't let her down and that I was only a phone call away if the current locksmith let them down. A day later she rang me for a job. I did it within the hour. Believe it or not, I now do five real estate branches for the same agent in five different suburbs. So, even when your mind tells you to give up or it's too hard, have a go. You might be surprised where this gets you.

I'm a good example that education is not important in starting and having a go in business. If you think you can't do it, think again. If I can, you can too. Starting a business is tough. I learnt the hard way and have a lot of valuable lessons to pass on to others who might be thinking about starting a business, or who are already in business and need some help. So, if you would like to contact me at any stage and would like to ask me any questions about how I did it, please email me at justin@ toplock.net.au

Invest in Yourself

Jamie Thomas

Jamie and his wife Vanessa are the owners of the marketing and design agency Synkd (pronounced: sink'd) based in northern Melbourne. Jamie is the Brand and Marketing Specialist, while Vanessa is the Creative Director.

As a marketer my ultimate goal is to help business owners to achieve 'financial freedom' and 'lifestyle' in their busy lives. It's the same goal that we at Synkd also aim for. No, I'm not a financial planner or a life coach. We help business owners achieve 'lifestyle' by promoting and growing successful businesses through the development and implementation of marketing strategies designed to convert customers, increase your brand awareness, generate large profits and produce return on your investment.

Essentially we get your business working for you instead of you working for your business! This in turn frees you up to choose whether you want to work or have to work. It's all about options.

My overriding passion (apart from Madagascan vanilla gourmet ice cream) is helping business people – specifically business owners – to 'stand out from the crowd' by identifying and developing commercially viable ideas that communicate clear, succinct marketing messages.

In the industry we define this as communicating your unique selling point or simply asking, What's different about your business? The aim is to 'get through' to your audience with tailored messages that resonate emotionally with your niche market. We do this in order to convert suspects (or non-believers) of your business into qualified leads or, ideally, 'raving fans'.

Born in England, I have lived in 'Marvellous Melbourne' since 2005 with Vanessa. She is the second-generation

Aussie daughter of two Italian immigrants who came to make a new life in Australia in the 1960s. That makes me a new-wave immigrant and I now consider myself to be an official 'hybrid Aussie' – I own a beer fridge after all.

Synkd: the story so far …

Synkd was formed from the creative concept of Vanessa Thomas. Her love and appetite for all things design and branding led her to gain extensive experience (both good and bad) of the design world from a number of leading Melbourne design agencies. The secret to Vanessa's success is clarity. She knew from day one exactly what she wanted to do in life – to design, to create, to produce. Graphic design – the use of words and imagery to create engaging visual messages for commercial success or profit (or to use the term coined by a strategic partner: 'she makes things look pretty') – was Vanessa's passion. Being the Italian that she is, nothing was going to prevent her from achieving her dreams and objectives.

Vanessa cut her teeth working for a number of high profile design clients, including the City of Melbourne Council, but the time soon came to jump off the employee safety net and go it alone. (Scary of course, but with hindsight it was more risky not to break out and do it for herself considering the growing uncertainty of job security.)

All she had, aside from creative ideas and a lone Mac computer, was a burning desire, an entrepreneurial streak and a determination to establish her own design agency, find her own clients and provide quality creative design solutions.

In another sense, Vanessa was entirely unique – this local girl from Thomastown, Melbourne, loved to create unique visual solutions and wanted to make something of herself. Sometimes that's all it takes to realise a dream – determination that is mixed with a drive and a passion.

Slowly but surely, Vanessa built up a small client base on a part-time basis. She managed her time and learnt as she went until she was able to 'grow it alone'. How? She used a number of growth strategies to help build her profile – she blitzed the networking scene morning, noon and night (I didn't see her for a month), attended structured, regular local networking groups (the BNI network and Business Chicks) to build a trusted network and forge a reputation for delivering design solutions. She branded herself correctly and, importantly, she applied for every council tender, which would prove to be a smart move – working to her business strengths and leveraging off her previous experience for the City of Melbourne Council. It has opened doors for Synkd.

In small business it's good to know your weaknesses but don't look to improve them – instead, delegate those weaker skills so you can focus on your strengths. Always focus on what you're good at as that's where your results and growth will come from.

The breakthrough came at the first-ever networking event that Vanessa attended. Her first client was a local primary school who required flyers, promotions and event tickets. Having quoted for the job, for both design and print management, it was a nervous week's wait for the school committee to reach a decision. Thankfully it came through positive and since then she's never looked back.

Three and a half years later and Synkd has secured placement on the panel of five top local metropolitan Councils (and we've applied to two more at the time of writing); we have a range of small to medium-sized businesses as a valued client base who provide regular, repeat work; and we're even more ambitious to grow and produce highly creative designs for clients.

Jamie's story:

My story is the typical corporate drone story that many have experienced and told with a look of dread in their eyes – of working for and through the system, putting the hours in, delivering results for clients but sacrificing much in the process. The biggest sacrifices are freedom and time for the family, predicaments many of us find ourselves in these days.

I guess the real difference comes down to those who are brave, willing or crazy enough to risk it all for a better life. My part in the overall strategy involved providing Synkd with the platform, the breathing space and the opportunity for Vanessa to go out and grow the business by covering most of the living expenses.

Professionally, I had reached the corporate crossroads and needed to make a decision.

My experience in the advertising industry amounts to a total of ten years, broken up into two parts: five years of design industry experience as a graphic designer for various design studios and architectural groups, with five years of additional marketing experience as a marketer/account manager for a range of blue chip corporate client accounts. So the benefit our clients receive is design and strategic marketing skills from the one brain!

I'd been responsible for the account management, implementation and delivery of marketing and printed advertising collateral for 3 years on the V/Line regional railways account, producing state-wide train timetable collateral for the state of Victoria – attention to detail is key and, frankly, my eyesight has never recovered.

It was a great experience and one where I learnt the importance of meeting a deadline, time management, the importance of aligning yourself strategically with clients, working both individually and within a team as well as providing superior customer service to build trust and keep those clients coming back. These are all key strategies when working in small business.

Moving on from V/Line, I was responsible for driving the account of German brand Miele premium white goods for Australian and New Zealand territories. This involved the implementation of national marketing strategies and monthly campaigns that included media buying, strategic planning, development, production and delivery of TV commercials, radio ads, press ads, point of sale and digital media/web content.

More responsibilities and increased pressure came with the territory, but I thrived on the pressure and the tight turnarounds. Campaigns were rolled out continuously over consecutive months and I enjoyed the range and scope of the job. Media buying, understanding the world of TV and radio networks and implementation of creative strategy were my core competencies on this account.

Eventually I moved upwards to the Volkswagen Commercial Vehicles Australia corporate account, which now offered full suite national advertising campaign experience and provided full scope advertising from outdoor signage, to national TV and press advertisements, retail signage and digital/online media content. For me this was almost the golden chalice of corporate blue-chip integrated and multi-channel marketing strategy roles. I said 'almost'.

It was a great opportunity and a great challenge where I learnt a lot about the industry, about integrated multi-channel marketing campaigns and also about myself.

Altogether, what I gained was real-world marketing experience in a range of sectors spanning corporate, automotive, transportation, government, finance, health, superannuation, retail, and property development. Armed with all that experience, I'm now focused on developing effective marketing strategies combined with design creative for our own corporate and SME clients at Synkd.

There were a number of reasons why I considered my position and future as an employee. The realisation that job security simply didn't exist was one major factor. Turnover is normal in the advertising world. However, being at the mercy of someone else's business decisions didn't sit well with me. We were no strangers to adversity either – 5 years earlier and two weeks after settling on the mortgage for our first home loan I was fired without warning. It taught me to roll with the punches and to never to leave yourself open.

The second factor is that for the most part as an employee you're just another number. No matter how hard you work, or how many hours you put in, you are replaceable and soon forgotten. That's not bitterness, it's just the way it is. I soon understood that I wanted my efforts to benefit me directly – not someone else.

So if you're reading this and seriously contemplating breaking into business for yourself just consider those realities and always make an informed decision.

I was brought up on the belief that you make yourself indispensable, that you look to add value in whatever ventures you're in. This same work ethic was instrumental in reaching the heights of working on the Volkswagen account but – after a five-year marathon of marketing deadlines and design deliveries with not much downtime – the time had come to make a choice. To be honest I wasn't enjoying the role anymore and if anything it had become too demanding and had taken over my life. With a young family to support you naturally start to question your role and what you're prepared to sacrifice. I wasn't 21 any more. I was torn between choosing a career and providing for the family – so I chose both!

In the end the choice was relatively simple. On one hand it was stay put, play it safe, continue to work for the 'man', sacrifice your time to keep a roof over your family's head and keep your head above water with a young, growing family (baby number two was on the way). And on the other hand, it was risk it all, break free, throw off the corporate shackles and do it for yourself, take control of your destiny and at the same time your financial future. Which would you choose?

In the marketing world we have a term for it – it's fittingly entitled a 'call to action'. It simply means you need to take some kind of action but sometimes that's the hardest part of all. You start to feel the fear. When that happens, you do it anyway.

The choices we have made have ultimately changed the future for our lives and the lives of our two-year-old son Nathan and one-year-old daughter Mia. It's our one motivation and we're determined to make Synkd a success. (Yes, that's right – two kids within 13 months of each other, and building a brand new business together with your partner. Admittedly it's not great timing but ask yourself when is it really a good time to start a business?)

Its funny – sometimes you don't truly realise at the time the true implications of the big decisions you make in life. Giving it your best shot combined with laser focus are, I believe, two key qualities that determine success in business.

The straw that broke the camel's back was caused ultimately because I didn't see my daughter for the first week of her life – too 'busy' servicing clients and helping my employers sell 'units'. It put things into perspective and for the first time challenged my priorities as a father and a provider. Yet another hard life lesson learnt!

I'd come across a saying that was applicable to modern life that goes like this: in order to be successful you should 'do the opposite to everyone else'.

Who was I to argue?

I walked away from a highly demanding, yet regular (read: married to the job), 'safe' (so long as I was meeting performance indicators, deadlines and sales figures), half-decent paying corporate marketing job. The downside of that job was a 70-plus hour week, the challenge of managing a team of eight Gen Y staff, combined with an all-round three-hour commute. I traded it all in to join up with my significant other in her three and a half year old graphic design business 'adventure'. Any regrets? Well, I don't miss that commute!

At Synkd I found myself with no resources, no support, and no regular paycheque, but on the plus side, thankfully, no major debt. We'd kept living expenses low as a result of the GFC and we hadn't over-extended ourselves with mortgage stress. Granted we were in a better position than most but we had little, if any, savings.

Why leave a relatively comfortable corporate job and risk it all? Freedom and lifestyle. Freedom is my underlying motivation and reason for starting in business. To ultimately have the freedom to do what I want, when I want – as well as to achieve financial freedom for the family.

In order to achieve this financial independence we had noticed a familiar trend: that most financially successful people all had businesses of their own and they all had their 'money machine' working for them – independent entities, self-sufficient, future proof (to a degree). It was a pretty obvious choice – easy in theory, of course.

Reality is a little different.

It'll take time but at Synkd we have a creative plan and with a clear focus we know we'll reach our objectives. The importance of fixed goals is paramount in business and we now have them established.

Overnight, late in March 2013, Synkd morphed quietly and with little fanfare into Synkd: Marketing & Design. With the first rule of marketing broken (make a noise), the two disciplines formed into a congruent partnership and we were on our way.

Ironically enough, at Synkd I ended up working harder, for longer hours and for next to no pay, so not much of a deal but with one huge difference – we stopped being pushed along by life. We had taken control and I was happy to have a bit more balance.

I now saw my kids every morning and evening. The in-laws helped us out, which underlines just how important the support of extended family has been for Synkd's success to date. Getting family and friends buy-in can really help in business! (Sometimes, of course, it doesn't always work out that way but doubters should only spur you on.)

It was inspiring knowing that you get out of business exactly what you put in. All of your hard work and dedicated hours pay off when it works for your own business, instead of working harder and earning dollars for someone else. That was a really strong motivating force.

Originating from the north west of England, I inherited a pretty strong work ethic, a strong sense of justice and fair play, a strong accent, and a big antidote to stop me from getting too big for my boots. Very much an 'adopted Aussie' mentality in many ways – so a home away from home (apart from the weird sport the locals called 'football').

The part of the world that I came from – very alien to Melbourne in many ways but also similar in others – is a hard place to survive. Unfortunately, entrepreneurship and preparation for success in the business world isn't high on the school curriculum in Merry Olde England, so a sharp learning curve was the order of the day.

Despite this, I'd always understood the value in investing in education and continuous learning. A short business course laid the foundation for a basic understanding of running a business. Training prepared me for the challenge.

In business it's all about building a network, promoting the business, looking for opportunities to demonstrate our expertise in marketing and design and helping businesses to differentiate from the competition. Do this well and continue to do this and you'll be streets ahead of your competitors.

How have we found success?

Invest in yourself – if budget and time allows (note: make time) enrol in a short business course before venturing out alone so that you understand those key business principles.

I completed a small business course through Swinburne TAFE, which really helped open my eyes to the core principles of business. It's definitely worth the investment and it will stand you in good stead for future success. Having the awareness and knowledge – despite the lack of real experience – is invaluable for making those important early business decisions.

Learn the basics like 'cash flow is king', the importance of the profit and loss and balance sheet, necessary legislation and bookkeeping skills (aim to delegate wherever possible), how to set up a business, an appropriate business name and how to register it and secure an online presence, operational and staffing/HR issues, branding and marketing – those who know me better know I could go on … but I won't.

Too many people adopt the Fields of Dreams mentality: 'If I build it they will come'. They think they can just set up a business on the advice of family and friends (who always mean well and won't tell you how it really is). They open the doors and expect that the world will simply rush in and 'buy them'. It doesn't quite work that way in the real world.

Don't get me wrong, customers do 'buy' you, but budding business owners do need to learn how to sell – it's the one skill you need to master.

Reading Kiyosaki and books like E-myth really helped increase our collective knowledge and exposure of business before Synkd actually made those first tentative steps. Educating ourselves about money and what it means to different people also opened our eyes and minds to the different ways of looking at and conducting business.

Learning how to generate profitable ventures, building a strong internal brand culture and creating a team of passionate, like-minded people are also key concepts that we'll look to bring into the structure at Synkd.

Know your customer as well as you can and build up a detailed profile so that you know them inside and out – often referred to as your Avatar (it's encouraged to name your Avatar too!). Find out what your customers like about you, what they don't like, why they buy from you, what they buy, when they buy and, importantly, how they would like to buy!

Gather as much information as you can on your customers – it all helps to understand and get into their minds. By putting yourself in their shoes you'll be more aware of the purchasing and buying process from your customer's point of view. **Extra Tip**: Aim to improve this 'conversion and sales funnel' wherever possible and you'll see your leads increase!

By the way, this information is completely free (apart from investing your time)! All you have to do is ask your customers for feedback – preferably when they've made a successful purchase. Many business owners simply don't engage with their customers.

The rules in marketing have changed and the aim in business now is to convert your customers and make them the 'brand ambassadors' of your business so they refer for you. The way I figure it, if the big corporate guys can do it, then so can you!

Why don't some business owners ask for feedback? Maybe it's fear of personal rejection, or a fear of bringing a negative element to their customers' attention that might prove detrimental to their current offering? Ask yourself this: how are you going to improve your business's offering if you don't hit the big issues on the chin? Be brave enough to ask those difficult questions as part of your continuous improvement policy to customer service. By all means make the necessary changes and see client retention skyrocket. What's more you'll gain goodwill and trust by improving your core service. It's a win/win scenario for all.

As I am often heard to say, marketing will get you customers but only good customer service will keep them!

Benefits not features! Review your unique selling point and make sure you clearly communicate the benefits of your business/service or product.

Your customers don't buy detergent; they buy clean and soft clothes. My clients don't buy marketing strategies and design services from me; they buy improved brand awareness, greater conversions, increased sales and higher profits.

When you stop and think about it, people hire you because of what you believe – that's to say what you can do for them, not what you actually do. I appreciate that this might sound a bit confusing, but if you think about it, you'll find that it's true.

You don't go to the local shopping centre and buy a mattress; you buy a good night's sleep. You don't just buy a wheel or a clutch from a mechanic; you buy convenience, efficiency, a reliable ride, mobility, or status depending on your consumers' mindset or specific needs. This philosophy holds true in any business regardless if it's online or offline. If you're running a small business, remember this and build your marketing around it as it will really make or break your marketing spend.

Focusing on what your company does rather then what the end result is for the customer will not only hurt your sales, but your branding will suffer as well.

Why is this? Here's the fun psych part: because fundamentally your customers buy benefits, not features. And benefits invoke emotional responses. Since we're all mostly human we all make our purchases based on emotional and motivational forces. We tend to post-rationalise our purchases in a vain attempt to justify our emotional impulses. As a result we try to deny that we're all slaves to our own emotional states, which is where the dreaded buyer's remorse comes from.

Always remember that your clients or customers come back to you because of what you can give to them (the benefits or the added value) but they're not that interested in how you achieve this (the features).

My last tip for business owners? Exploit this strategy for all it's worth and make sure that the benefits are what you talk about in your marketing and copywriting. That way your customers will always understand the value of what you offer and they'll be more likely to keep coming back for more.

Visit synkd.com.au if you'd like a chat or for more information about standing out from the crowd.

Learn From Your Mistakes

Melissa Baker

A mother of three, Melissa is the director of Enrichment Property Group and Mel Baker Property Management.

I would never have had the courage to venture out on my own and be my own boss without the support and encouragement of my best friend – my husband. It takes a lot of guts to take that leap of faith and hope you don't fall flat on your face. In my early 20s, I made my first attempt to be my own boss when I was presented with an opportunity to run a florist inside an already established nursery. I had been working as a florist for 12 months, so I thought, Hey, why not? I know how to make flower arrangements.

I made so many mistakes at first, like over-ordering stock and poor marketing. I didn't have a clue about how to bring customers in, and I made a loss every week until I finally gave up and quit.

Several years later, another opportunity arose for me to run a cleaning business for bulk building companies where there was a housing boom; my job was to do the final clean before the clients moved into their brand new home. I became known for my quality of work and I decided I needed help, so I employed 3 staff and paid them a set amount per job and provided them with all the cleaning equipment. For 18 months we flew, the business was doing really well, but it seemed the more staff I employed to help the less money I made. Although I chose to finish up the cleaning business I was very grateful that it introduced me to the love of property.

Not long afterwards, I began my career in real estate and job shared a part-time position for a couple of years whilst my two boys weren't at school. I met my husband, who had also been working in real estate for many years, and it wasn't long before we decided to venture out on our own.

I worked alongside him as the business manager. I was in charge of managing staff, office administration, training and overseeing the operation of the business. I also fell pregnant within the first year of our new business, which was – to say the least – a little challenging.

Together, we ran the business for 5 years. We had some great times, great staff, but we were a newly married couple with a new baby and 5 children between us. Understandably, we were exhausted.

We both love real estate and couldn't imagine doing anything else, so we decided to create a niche business, and Enrichment Property Group was born.

Our initial mandate was that we're your 'one-stop shop' to real estate. Whether it is selling the family home, managing your investment property, or creating wealth through property development, you will receive the very best in skills and service. We also understand the importance of quality and realistically priced property services in ensuring your financial independence.

In the first six months I was extremely busy, but also very excited at the same time. I wanted to do everything at once. In hindsight, I would have been more productive had I created a checklist and worked through most important to least important tasks for that day. I was also extremely fearful of spending money in the beginning, and because I started out with very little capital I was very conservative in the way I spent. I only bought small quantities of letterhead, business cards, stationery, etc.

In a real estate business, cash flow is sporadic, so you have to learn to budget and not get caught up in all the bells and whistles when it comes to things like websites, email addresses, Google ad words, etc. I felt like I was constantly bombarded by marketing and sales people, but after six months of trading the cash flow became more consistent and I was able to worry less about money.

I decided that I would work from home until I had established myself and determine if I really needed an office. I lasted five months like this, and although I would spend most of my time on the road or at appointments, it simply wasn't working for a number of reasons. Amongst them:

- I found it extremely difficult to separate work and home life.

- I was rapidly running out of space and my 'work space' was always cluttered and untidy.

- I was spending too much time driving around to meet with people.

The obvious choice was to find an office. There is nothing better than being at work and walking out at the end of the day, closing the door behind you. Mentally your brain is telling your body, *Work is finished for the day, now let's focus on family or catching that movie tonight.*

Another reality was that the business wasn't going to grow substantially without having an office and separate space to meet with clients.

The added advantage of having the office is that there is more than enough room to sub-let to another tenant should we ever need to, but it's amazing how you manage to find ways to fill the space.

The business is now 2 years old and I also have two admin support staff on a permanent part-time basis. Having run an office of 10 staff in the past, I knew it was necessary to appoint admin staff from the outset. Being able to delegate administration work allowed me more time to work on my business and better service my clients.

My admin staff work school hours; they are very good at their job, but they also want to be available for their children. As a mum, I understand and know it is difficult to find an employer who will give you the flexibility to take half a day off to attend your son's sports carnival or leave work after 1 hour because childcare has called as your baby has a temperature. I understand because this was me early in our business. It didn't mean I wouldn't work my butt off once I was back at work, and that is exactly the same with my staff.

I can't stress the point enough: value your staff as much as they value you. Your staff will come and go, and although they are integral to your business whilst they work for you, they will eventually move on. In my experience, they are extremely loyal and hardworking when you treat them well.

I also try to involve my staff in all aspects of the business so they understand my expectations. Simple things like changing fresh flowers each week and lighting the candle for the oil burner first thing in the morning makes them aware that they play a part in the overall success of the business. I trust my staff 110% and I can only put that down to:

- Good, honest relationships.

- Mutual respect and showing appreciation – at the end of every day I personally thank my staff for all they have done.

- Remembering to have fun! Work doesn't feel like work when you enjoy what you do. We are social beings. I think it's important to take the time to share a coffee and chat. I see it as an investment.

As our business has grown, it also evolves. Over the last 2 years, we have noticed we have been able to create some niche services. By creating a niche, you eliminate the competition because fewer companies will offer the same service.

Our specialty is to provide a broader prospective on investing. As you read this book it would be great for you to think about what your speciality is and what you can provide that is unique to the marketplace.

In alignment with our broader business strategies we also understand the importance of communicating more simplistic areas of our business. An example of this is the establishment of our sister business Mel Baker Property Management. This ensures that potential clients seeking a "back to basics" property service are catered for, and it also introduces them to our broader business. It is important to listen to your market to ensure that your business continually evolves and you focus on providing the service that is in demand.

My Top 10 Business Tips

1. Make sure you find your niche in the market place, otherwise you will be just the same as everyone else. What is your point of difference? What can you offer that others can't? Once you know what your niche is, teach others around you to do what you do, otherwise you're simply buying yourself a job.

2. Have a clear purpose for your business. Set goals and make yourself accountable to them or you could end up with a business with no direction. As Steven Covey says, 'Begin with the end in mind.'

3. Start the day by conquering the most difficult task first, and then spend the rest of the day working on dollar-productive tasks. We have a habit of spending a lot of our day keeping 'busy' but when we really think about it, if there is no financial upside to what we're doing then we should stop doing it.

4. If you receive a lot of voice messages during the day, dedicate a specific time every day to return them rather than distracting from the task at hand. I find the best time to return calls is in the car between appointments. I'm surprised by how much time this frees up.

5. Set aside two specific times in your day to answer emails. Today, with email at our fingertips 24/7, it's too easy to fall into the trap of answering emails the moment we receive them. I find if you can make

a conscious effort to stick to this, you will more than likely answer emails efficiently and get more out of your day. If you're like me and receive a lot of emails, this habit also helps ensure you don't forget any!

6. Education is an ongoing lesson. As my husband says quite regularly, 'Every day is a school day'. It's one of the most important investments we can make in our businesses; I don't think we can ever stop learning. In real estate law, legislation is often changing and it's so important that I am educating my clients and that they are aware of their legal obligations. Staff training is equally as important, as it can refresh and enhance their skills, and keep them efficient and interested.

7. Don't be scared of making mistakes, but, if possible, learn from the mistakes of others.

That's what this book is about.

8. Surround yourself with people who are smarter than you. Good service providers such as accountants, financial advisors and solicitors are invaluable in the world of business. Join a networking group. Networking with other business owners has greatly assisted me with my business success.

9. Overestimating and under delivering. When we start out in business we have a tendency to underestimate our costs and overestimate our potential income. I'd like to challenge new business owners to run a parallel budget that overestimates costs and underestimates income. Can your business sustain months where the alternative budget is reality? And don't forget to put your salary down as what you're really worth rather than the minimum wage,

even if you don't necessarily pay that to yourself for the first few months.

10. Have fun! We run our own business because we want the freedom, flexibility and income that come with being self-employed. We can choose to enjoy what we do and smile when things get tough or we can become a victim of self-employment where we hate what we do and blame everyone else for our failures. If you don't think it's fun anymore, and you stop believing in what you offer, then go and get a job!

Recognise and Seize Opportunity

Steven Briffa

Since 1993, Steven Briffa has been the owner and director of Plenty Valley Printing.

I left school at the end of Year 11 and bummed around for a year or two before getting a job as a driver for a medical laboratory. During my spare hours as a driver I began to help out in other areas of the laboratory. My employer saw potential in me and suggested I go back to school as a mature-aged student and I went on to complete a Diploma in Applied Science in Medical Laboratories at RMIT University.

Upon completion I was promoted to a laboratory technician. I was the owner's first employee, but over the six and a half years I was there the lab grew from a team of three people to over 140 staff members. As the lab grew so did I. I became well-respected for my work ethic and my contributions to helping all areas excel. It was an ideal job but still there was something missing.

I wanted to be my own boss.

The video industry had begun to boom and I decided that this would be wise to invest in. I purchased a video shop in Preston. However, I was unaware that the industry was undergoing major changes with franchises taking over.

One year after I had purchased the business with borrowings of over $120,000 from the bank, sales gradually dropped. Initially we were making around $3500 per week. Now we were just getting around $1200 per week. I started to panic. I had no idea where to go from here but it looked like eventually we were going to go down.

I decided to get a full-time job during the day and have my wife manage the video shop in the hopes that an extra wage would keep us afloat. I got a job at Snap Printing in Footscray. At the end of each day I would go and take over the video shop from my wife so that she could then attend to our home duties. Although this seemed like a good plan the video shop turnover and my wage from Snap Printing were still not enough to cover the video shop's debt.

We struggled like this for two years. It was only when my wife fell pregnant with our first child that the decision to sell became eminent. We hoped that selling the business was the best option and would pay off some of our debt quickly. What we didn't take into consideration was that no one wanted to buy a business that was losing money. We decided to just close up and sell everything. We paid the bank what we could and negotiated a new payment plan based on my full-time wage at Snap Printing.

I did buy into a café in North Melbourne with a friend to try and get my dream of owning my business rolling again but I had little business knowledge. I ended up getting ripped off and losing money I didn't really have in the first place.

Money was scarce and my wage just covered my bank repayments and some food for my family. My wife and I had a rule: pay the bills first, and then make sure we had enough food for our daughter, and then make sure we had food. It wasn't the best way to live but we had support from family members who would show up with parcels of food. As this was going on, I was working full-time at Snap and doing odd jobs part time. I was exhausted, but we were surviving.

I worked like this for a few years and then we found out we had another child on the way.

I had just finished working a full week at Snap. I had also worked a few nights tiling with my brother in-law that week and was looking forward to some extra cash from my Saturday job. My wife drove me to work from Garden City, Port Melbourne to Errol Street, North Melbourne. My uncle owned a café and I had become a dishwasher there, working 9.00 am until 5.00 pm every Saturday.

My wife dropped me off and then drove away. I walked into work. My uncle looked at me and came straight over to have what I thought was going to be a friendly chat. He then explained that my services were no longer required as they had to cut back their wages. I thought he was joking. After he led me outside I realized that this was no joke. I had lost my job. I had no money in my pocket to get home and I was too embarrassed to go back into the café and use the phone to call my wife to pick me up, so I started walking home, wondering why life was treating me so badly. I walked along the old docklands area with tears streaming down my face.

Feeling totally confused I stopped and looked around and realised I had been going through life without a plan, and due to this I had ended up in this situation, financially unstable and in debt. Instead of giving up on my dream, though, I decided to change my plans.

More importantly, I decided to change my mindset.

I was going to set goals and have a timeline for achievements. I needed to continue to work my arse off and set myself up with my own part-time business. I had experienced pain and suffering but without it I wouldn't have been able to learn and see the path I needed to take.

I continued to walk home, still distraught from being sacked and my face and eyes bright red from all the crying but with a plan and idea, a vision of where I wanted to be.

When I arrived home, my wife instantly knew our bad luck had struck again. She asked what had happened and if I had done something wrong. Even though I was upset I explained this needed to happen so that we could move forward.

I told her how we needed to buy a small foil printing machine and start doing jobs from home to make extra money. I saw there was a market for foil printing as Snap Printing used off-site print brokers to complete foil jobs. She nearly fell over when I spoke about spending one full week's pay on a machine to try and make money. After long discussions she knew it was the right step forward, but how could we afford to spend one full week's pay on a foil machine that I had no idea how to run? On top of that, where would the work come from?

Not only did we need to put aside one week's wage to purchase a small bench top foiling machine but I needed to learn how to use it. I knew of a person in Pascoe Vale who specialised in foil printing so I volunteered my time and services on the weekends and in return he taught me how to work the machine. To this day we are still good friends. He taught me many aspects of foil printing and also how to operate different print machines, including a commercial guillotine.

Now I was picking up a few odd jobs for myself on behalf of Snap Printing and over a six month period I printed everything from business cards to fridge magnets. Although I wasn't making much money I was earning a reputation amongst other Snap owners as the go-to man when it came to foil printing.

I had a deal with a couple of Snap stores that, after hours, I could see their clients when they had enquiries about foil printing. This helped me to hone my sales skills because I was forced to sell myself and my product at a discounted rate. This meant that Snap Printing stores still got credit for my hard work, but I was able to make a small commission on the side.

The plan was to be able to print two or three jobs per week and I would be able to support my family. But I found that the more I learnt about foil printing the more I wanted to learn about other areas within the printing field. I started volunteering my services to a larger local commercial printer who I had met through Snap Printing. Now my Saturdays were taken up working on larger equipment and understanding the principles of advanced printing.

He loved the fact that I was working for nothing and he took full advantage of how much work I could get through within a day. This was a short term plan for me as my true goal was to continue building my own clientele. Although he used me to further his business production, I was using him to further my own.

I had now established a few regular clients of my own and was making a small amount of money from my foil printing. I reinvested that money into stock and a small offset printing press. Off-Set Printing was Snap's speciality but in order to sustain my own business and maintain some financial stability I had no choice but to move into this area. I was careful to never approach any of Snap's clients and friends of mine who were using Snap continued to do so because it would have been obvious if they had all moved across to my services.

I got a big break through a friend to print for a large accounting firm. They had constant orders and this would keep me busy most nights. I eventually lost that client as they discovered I was working from home. In their eyes I was not reputable enough to complete the work required, as I was a backyard operator, someone they did not want to be associated with.

Some weeks later a good friend of mine who was a printing press engineer asked me if I could help out his friend who owned a small print shop in Greensborough. He needed help because all of his staff had walked out on him. I didn't think to ask why as I saw the potential to make some additional money. I already had a few small jobs but I can never say no.

The owner was a nice chap, a bit vague but nice. When we negotiated an hourly rate I was determined to get a minimum of $20.00 cash per hour. Before I could state my desired rate he offered $25.00 an hour. I was quick to say yes.

I began working for him and after the first day I practically ran the place. He gave me the keys and told me that he would book the jobs in and I could print, trim and pack all the work on Saturdays and Sundays. He would deliver and book in more work during the week for the following weekend. That all sounded good so off we went. I worked ten hours on the Saturday and eight hours on Sunday, a cool $450.00 for the weekend. I was pretty impressed with myself.

As he didn't come in on Sunday I had to wait until the following Saturday to get paid. That wasn't a problem though. The following Saturday I showed up and started work early. He popped in around 11.00am and sat around for a while and then disappeared. I worked all day Saturday and then Sunday. This went on for five weeks and I also did a couple of additional nights during the week because we were falling behind and my main concern was making sure he didn't let customers down as he had no idea how to actually print or trim work.

At this stage I hadn't been paid at all for my five weeks of service and was pretty desperate to get paid. I called him on the

Friday and said that it was important that we chat in the morning. He agreed.

I arrived at 6.00 am and started work as usual. He arrived around 10.00 am and we sat down and began chatting. I was pretty busy and there were a number of jobs to get through so I cut to the chase and asked when I could get my money. The expression on his face instantly changed. He dropped his head into his hands and said that if I wanted my money he had no choice but to close the doors on Monday as he was broke.

I said he must be kidding, we had plenty of work going through so where was the money? That's when he opened up and explained he was paying his debts, which were large and he was a long way in arrears. My response was, 'What about me?'

I went down to the kitchen to settle down and make a cup of tea. I thought back to my defining moment and when all looked lost. I started thinking clearly. All I had to do was look at the situation again but from a different angle.

This was my opportunity.

I approached him and asked how much he wanted for a walk-in-walk-out sale of the business. He started thinking about it and we agreed on $15,000, less what he owed me.

I was going to take over Monday morning and he no longer had to worry about the rent or the responsibility of producing any work. He was an accountant and not a printer. He would pay his suppliers what he could and start working for a friend to pay off the remaining debts.

Monday morning came and I organised for my wife to hand over the cheque. We had raised the money by talking to the bank and getting some help from a relative. For the first week, my wife and I came up with a couple of lines for anyone who called to explain that we were taking over and the turnaround would be slow for the next two weeks until I came on full time. The next day I put in my notice at Snap. My boss, a friend for many years, asked me to leave effective immediately.

I was now a business owner of a small print shop in the back streets of Greensborough and had to get my act together very quickly. The turnover had been approximately $2,000–$2,500 per week for the last twelve months. However, with my new ideas, calling every client we had on file, and also working our way through the classifieds, during week one and two we turned over between $4,000–$5,000 per week.

With every client we called we explained my print background and asked them to give us a chance and we would not let them down. Communication and service beyond expectation was the key to our success.

We put our prices up as the previous prices were ridiculously low and we justified this with quality, service and the fact that our clients could rely on us. This combination worked for us then and is still working for us today.

I have owned Plenty Valley Printing since 1996 and still enjoy working incredible hours and dealing with a wide range of clients from all around Australia. To this day I still own my first foil printing machine. It serves as a constant reminder of where I came from and how hard it was back in those days.

We have relocated twice since taking over and now operate from a 500-square metre fully modernised building purposely built for the quick print industry, with eight full-time staff members. Our digital equipment combined with our knowledge of the industry has given me a life that I could have never imagined possible for a kid who had no plans for the future and dropped out of school after Year 11.

Things To Live By in Business

- People don't plan to fail in business, they just fail to plan

- I don't expect my staff to do anything that I am not prepared to do myself

- Deliver a service above your customer expectation

- Always live within your means, especially while building your business

- Don't try and keep up with the Joneses because most of the time they are struggling to keep up with the other Joneses

- Massive pain is the key factor that helps you see your pathway

- When people around me say that I am so lucky, I think back and often say, 'The harder I work the luckier I seem to get.'

Engage People Through Your Story

Blaise van Hecke

*Busybird Publishing is a small business
located in Montmorency, Victoria, headed
by the dynamic husband and wife team,
illustrator and photographer Kev Howlett, and
writer, editor and designer Blaise van Hecke.*

If you visit the Busybird Publishing Studio Gallery, you will very soon be inspired to find out more about what publishing entails and how it can be empowering to give it a go. We like to think of it as a nest (sorry, it's cheesy, I know) that everyone wants to live in. Our staff members are qualified and passionate about publishing, too.

We live and breathe everything to do with words, images and ideas.

Busybird Publishing is all about helping people get their story into the world. It's said that everyone has at least one book in them. I would say that once a person publishes one book, they will find themselves hooked and embark on a publishing journey that can be very fulfilling, both financially and personally. This can be true no matter what type of book you write: memoir, business book, family history, novel or poetry collection. The list is only limited by your imagination.

Writing a book really is a creative project that will help you express yourself and your story to then connect with hundreds and thousands of people.

Think about this: the connection between a writer and a reader is like an intimate conversation. The time that a person spends to read a book (six, ten, fifteen hours, depending on length) is a chance for the writer to connect with that reader and have their undivided attention. Where else might you get that kind of situation between two strangers?

It's not hard to see, then, why our business is passionate about creating these situations between a writer and a reader. We offer publishing solutions for any type of book project and will guide a person from the very first seed of an idea to our favourite part: the book signing.

Nothing gives us more pleasure than working on a project with someone and being there at the launch to watch their beaming faces as they sign books. For many, it can be life changing.

In the past fifteen years in business, my partner, Kev, and I have made many mistakes. Most of these mistakes have been from ignorance about how to best run a business. We have been asked, 'But why didn't you ask for help?' My reply is, 'How can you ask a question when you don't know what the question is?'

Running your own business is fraught with dangers, and we've experienced a lot of them. We've often asked ourselves why we push on, because in fact we can both earn a good living as employees. But we live in an exciting age and we want to be part of the revolution. The digital era is changing the world of publishing (and many other industries) and opening up possibilities to so many people. This excites us and is the reason that we bound out of bed every single day to talk about books. Our business allows us to control our life, create our own destiny and create an uncapped income.

Kev and I met at photographic college in 1986, so it seems logical that we began our working life in photography. We didn't embark on our business enterprise, though, until we did the mandatory backpacking for 12 months. This was our test to see how well-suited we were for each other. As you can imagine, we came home with lots of photographs.

Busybird Publishing has taken many different forms. Before we focused on publishing, we offered just photographic services, then added illustration services. We had no real plans or goals and no idea about how to structure our business. Despite this, we managed to make decent money in the first eight years through a bit of luck and entrepreneurial thinking. We took advantage of advances in digital technology that allowed us to do work at half the cost offered in the marketplace but still make very good profits.

That journey started with a Mac G3 computer. Back then, it was expensive to buy a Mac but we bit the bullet, not knowing if the money we would make would justify the outlay. In other words, we didn't really have a business plan except to get the equipment needed (using a rental scheme) and set up an office in our dining room (back then, we had a nine square house and two small children!). We did have 'day' jobs. This meant that whatever income came from our business would be a bonus on top of our money as wage earners.

For anyone younger than, say, 40, think about this: in 1998, computers weren't in every household as they are now. Kev was working as an in-house photographer for a company, so he was computer literate. When we got our first Mac, I didn't even know how to turn it on, let alone send an email. If you don't know something, learn how to do it. I went to the local Living & Learning Centre and learnt basic email and desktop functions.

So investing in that computer and learning how to do the work was all that was really needed to make our business at that stage. Our business model was very simple: we set out to create hardcopy images into digital images for a business that created digital catalogues for the car industry. In a nutshell, we used a scanner and cleaned up the copy in Photoshop. This kept us in good cash flow for eight years. From time to time we said that we should look for other clients, but we had enough work for two of us and not really any idea how to add to our one-client list.

Guess what? The new technology superseded us after about ten years and the work went to China for about a third of what we were charging. We knew this would happen and had plenty of warning, so we decided to take a fresh look at our business. I went back to school to study publishing. By then, we had a house and an investment property and felt pretty secure.

Two things happened around this time. Both of us were working full-time in the business and we had a second investment property due to be built. But we had some personal issues. In a panic, we sold our house and the first property in order to be ready to settle the third property and divvy up our assets.

It could be that the emotional impact of our personal issues stopped us from thinking clearly. In hindsight, we should have gotten some financial advice in order to find a way to keep all three properties. We know now that this would've been possible.

We had some cash from the sale of our home, so we decided to invest in vending machines. We did do our due diligence and thought we had it all worked out. What we didn't account for was that vending machines are vandalised often. We owned three of them and soon realised that you need a large 'fleet' of them to really make a business out of it. After about 18 months, we sold the three damaged vending machines in frustration and at a loss.

By now, we were struggling to pay for the mortgage on our Richmond property and were rapidly going into debt. We decided to sell it and start fresh because the stress had become overbearing. Again, we didn't seek advice about another way to do it, as we might have been able to. We at least had no debt now, except that we had to pay capital gains on our property. This was disappointing because we sold it with very little profit. I'm sure that any accountant or financial planner would be shaking their head at some of the decisions that we made. Many of them were rash and emotion driven.

This brings me to something that I now tell people if they want to run their own business: do something you're passionate about. I talk to people about publishing and they come on board because of my passion. When those vending machines broke down or were vandalised, it was a frustrating hardship. We ended up loathing them. If something happens in our current business, we don't hesitate to ask for advice or seek solutions because we are doing something we love, something that we're good at and something that we know has big value.

We now have a thriving publishing business that is growing rapidly month-by-month and a product that we believe in. In a way, the business has come full circle and we are back to what we started doing: helping people tell their story. We have survived many ups and downs and learnt many lessons. To top it off, we are now 27 years married.

Fifteen years after the inception of Busybird, we feel like we're on solid ground. We have surrounded ourselves with people who give us good advice (and even offer solutions that we didn't know we needed) and we take care of business rather than just work in our business, which can end up feeling like just being an employee. It is hard work but doesn't feel like work; it is rewarding and it is exciting.

This is why I think that Kev and I are successful in business. We are still doing it after 15 years. Through all the ups and downs we haven't given up, because we believe in what we do and who we are. We just hadn't worked out how to do it. Now that we have worked out how to do it, and we know why we do it, it's just a matter of continuing to do it. For anyone in business or thinking about going in to business, I could give a list of tips, but here are my top three.

Creativity

When we talk about creativity, often people will say, 'Oh I'm not creative, I can't draw or write.' This isn't what I mean. Being creative in business means that when you come up against a problem you will come up with a solution to get you out of it.

Here's a small example: when we opened our studio, we didn't have a lot of cash flow, but we knew that signage was very important. We could only afford to pay for one side of a two-sided panel. This would have looked unsightly, so we decided to paint the other panel with blackboard paint and use it as a notice board until we could afford the other sign. That blackboard cost about $30 and has proven to be one of our best marketing tools and will not be replaced by a new sign.

Creativity comes into play for both financial problems as well as other business elements. Here's another small example: if your business has trouble with cash flow, as we have had, think creatively about how to get your clients to pay sooner or more often. In our business, some projects can cost up around $10,000. Even though we take a deposit, it can be a long time before we see the rest of the money. Some potential clients are put off about having to pay everything up front. The solution is to then create a payment plan over many months (or duration of project). This is a win-win situation. The client feels like they pay off the money (like a layby) and you have a stream of income rather than dealing in lump sums at long intervals.

My motto has become, 'There is a solution to every problem.' Sometimes it just takes a little creative thinking to find it.

Publish a Book

I wouldn't be in this business if I didn't think that publishing a book wasn't a good business decision. There are so many reasons why publishing is good for you. Besides being fun, it is like the ultimate business card and is very empowering (some might say life changing). You don't have to be an excellent writer. You have ideas, thoughts and experience in your head and there are many ways that you can get that into a book. You can improve your writing skills, dictate your book and transcribe it or get someone else (like me) to write it. Here are a few reasons why publishing a book is worth your while:

- You have 100% creative control

- Share your expertise

- Gain credibility in your field

- Gain trust by the marketplace

- Get more leads

- Grow your business

- Land speaking engagements

- Make money from book sales

- Create brand awareness

- Be known as an author

- Have fun!

Besides all of the above, writing a book is a good way for you to look very closely at what you do and find out how well you communicate that to the rest of the world. A book, after all, is a global product thanks to digital technology.

Publishing a book is a bit like a small business, so it's worthwhile getting the right people to help you. There are many pitfalls that can cost you money because of ignorance. But I guarantee that anyone who publishes their own book and does it the right way will make their money back very quickly and gain so much more. I promise that you will then be hooked on the process and will start a journey to last a lifetime.

Find Good People

It might take you a while to work out who is best for your business. If you don't like bookkeeping, then pay someone to do it. I did my own for many years and hated it. Back then it was fairly simple, with just one client, but now it has grown to a point that I cannot handle it and don't want to. I am more than happy for it to be done by a professional. There are many things that you can probably do in your business to save money – and early on you might have to – but in the end you will save money because you then have time to go out and gain more clients.

I find that this happens often in the publishing game. A client will come to me with their book and tell me that it has been edited and is ready to be published. I will read one page and realise that it's probably been edited by them or their wife or best friend. I will then tell them that I won't let them publish it at that quality because it will tarnish their reputation, as well as mine. For the cost of a few hundred dollars, you are protecting your asset. The same goes with photography. Yes, anyone can take a photo, but a professionally created image with the correct lighting can make a huge impact on the impression you give the world.

As well as getting the right people to help your business, you need to surround yourself with like-minded people in your business life. The best way to do this is through networking. I have always believed in networking but only started doing it consciously and actively a few years ago. It has made a huge difference to our business. By hanging out with other business owners, you learn from them and share your highs and lows. It is through networking that we have managed to find the right people to call on for our business needs, such as accountants, bookkeepers, insurance brokers, and the like. Surrounding yourself with other business owners also helps you keep motivated and accountable in your business.

Owning your own business is actually creating a lifestyle for yourself. It can be hard work and it can be frustrating, but if you set up your structures and systems it will get easier as your name becomes known. For us, it's about having ideas and being able to run with them rather than being kneecapped by company policy or budget restraints or even red tape. In our business, we come up with an idea, get excited and say, 'What a fantastic idea! Let's work out how to make it happen.'

Create Good Synergies

Paul Blake

Paul is a mortgage broker with the boutique finance broking company Citiwide Homeloans.

As a mortgage broker, I am the conduit between the client and the lender. My role is to handle the loan application, submit the loan to the bank, work with the lender to get the approval and then work with the client until the loan settles. Purchasing property is one of the most daunting prospects for clients, so my role is to make sure the transaction is as seamless as possible. Sure, problems can arise, but clients trust me for my ability to counter any issues that may arise to get the right outcome.

I specialise in both residential and commercial finance, where I deal with first homebuyers, people upgrading their property, as well as investors. I also assist clients who are looking for a better deal with their loan, or clients who are purchasing commercial property. A lot of businesses don't have the right products, whether they are loans, leases, accounts or eftpos terminals. I can work with clients to make sure that the bank is working for them rather than the other way around.

People use me for my experience – over 20 years in finance. I'm convenient too as I am fully mobile and contactable. Also, I think my greatest asset is problem solving, the ability to think on my feet and counter issues either before they arise or when they occur. I love what I do and still get a thrill when I am able to assist clients achieve their dreams.

How Did I Start?

I was not a great student, although not through want of trying. I became easily bored with school. It's hard as a parent now to tell my kids they need to study hard when I wasn't the model student. In my last two years of high school, I had no idea what I wanted to do. I loved fly-fishing but there was never any chance to make a living out of catching trout. I was also intrigued by journalism and politics, but my marks were never going to get me there. I nominated for university but I knew I'd better look for a job. Luckily, I passed VCE, which was a relief because I didn't want to fail. I had worked hard enough and that was more of a reward for my parents.

My dad was selling the ticket machines you see in delis where you take a number and when the number is displayed it is your turn. He was installing one in a bank, which was somewhat of a new idea for banks. I think he was concerned for me and he enquired with the person he was dealing with and was told to get me to submit a résumé. I did this and then was given an aptitude test, which I was concerned I might fail. Luckily I passed, had another interview and was then taken on by National Australia Bank. I don't know who was more relieved –

my family or me. I thought, *Stay with the bank for six months and then look for something else, maybe even do some more studies*. Twelve years later I was still with the bank and then decided to become a mortgage broker.

I did like my time with the bank. It definitely gave me the foundations for my business today – things like customer service, dealing with people, honesty and trust. During the latter years at the bank, I was doing home loans. I really loved assisting clients to purchase property and, as stated earlier, achieving their dream. During this time I also purchased my first home and it was an exciting time in my life.

Banks like to restructure, so after writing home loans for about 18 months, I was pushed into another role. While I didn't mind my new role, I was no longer doing home-loan lending. I wanted to get back into it, and mortgage broking had been around but had nowhere near the popularity that it has today. I was married and I had the support of my wife, so I decided to give it a go. Did I do the right thing? Looking back on it now, definitely. Have I made mistakes? Yes, but I have learnt so much in the last 12 years. I want to try and give you some tips to make sure your journey to becoming self-employed is a fun and profitable one.

Know Your Product

I understand this sounds pretty simple, but you need to present yourself as the expert in your field. I have 20 different lenders I deal with. Each lender has about six different products; that's about 120 odd loans and products. I don't know the ins and outs of every one of them, but what I make sure of is that I know at least three lenders and their products intimately. This enables me to help my client make choices, and if a client asks me a question I can confidently answer it. If for some reason I can't, I don't guess, I tell them, 'Look, I don't know the answer, I'll find out and come back to you.' If this happens to you, make sure you find the answer straight away and then get back to them. You don't want your client thinking that you don't know what you are doing.

Manage Your Time

Never turn up to an appointment late! I make sure that I am at the client's front door on time. If you are late, it doesn't make a good first impression. If I am travelling to a client's place and know that I am going to be ten minutes late or more (and it does happen, despite the best intentions), I will call them to tell them I am running late and apologise. This then shows that I am professional and also serious. You have agreed on a time with your client to meet, the client has made themselves available, so the least you can do is turn up on time.

My first client, 12 years ago, came about because they had made an appointment with another broker that didn't even turn up. I was on time; this meant I had the client already.

As part of time management, you need

to know how long each appointment is going to take. I allow one and a half hours and then travel time if I am booking back-to-back meetings. Don't overbook yourself; clients will understand if you can't see them for a couple of days. This can be hard if you're a tradie because you have to quote, do the actual job, and there are also emergencies in there as well. If you can manage your diary well, you are going to put yourself ahead of so many others, because so many arrive late or don't arrive at all.

Build a Synergy Group

I am sure other authors in this book will discuss networking. I find it invaluable. What I want to talk about is something different, and that is 'synergy groups'. When I first started mortgage broking, I worked out early on that I needed to have a group of experts that I could draw on if my clients required their services. With this in mind, I brought into my group an accountant, conveyancer, real estate agent, financial planner, leasing consultant and insurance broker. What this meant was that if a client was purchasing a property, I could pass on details of a conveyancer to them. If they were selling a property in my local area, I could forward details of a real estate agent. If they said to me, 'My accountant is not doing the right thing,' I could say, 'Here is an accountant who I can strongly recommend.' This makes you look like an expert in the eyes of your client. The upside of my group is that, whilst I refer them business, I get business in return. If you haven't got these sorts of contacts, go and do it. Imagine if you are a plumber and went to an electrician and said, 'Is it okay if I refer business to you?' What do you think they are going to say? They will feel obliged to give you business.

Please make sure that the people in your group will represent you in a professional manner. If you are giving out someone's details to a client of yours, you want to make sure they work to the same standards as you. If that person doesn't do the right thing, it will reflect poorly on you. It's not really a problem. I am sure someone else will be more than happy to receive referrals from you.

Get a Good Accountant

Your accountant needs to structure things correctly for you from day one. They will advise on whether you need a trust set up or a company. They will also discuss with you asset protection, and ultimately they complete your returns and try and minimise tax for you. They will be an invaluable asset to you as you navigate your way through business.

Just as importantly, accountants can be great referrers. The reason I say this is because clients run everything by their accountant. I'm obviously not an accountant, but they must be like therapists at times. They know if you get married, if you get divorced, if you are buying a property or if you are setting up a new business. Don't tell me they haven't got plenty of opportunity to refer business back to you.

Also, remember you will have opportunity to refer back to them. All your friends will tell you they have the best accountant. If they don't, there is your opportunity to refer them to your new best friend.

Get Buy-In From Your Family

If you're starting a business, your partner or family members need to be part of the journey. When I started, I made sure my wife was aware that I would be out after hours, that I may need to work weekends and even when on holidays. Sure, you do need to make time for yourself and your family, but remember your clients are depending on you and you don't want to let them down. There will be many ups and downs and you need to celebrate success, but more importantly your family members need to assist you when things aren't going your way and, trust me, things don't always go your way.

When you start, cash flow is going to be vital; you are going to need capital in order to start. Make sure you plan this before you start. When I started, my wife was working, so we knew that X amount was coming into the household every week and in order to survive I needed to make up the difference. As a couple, we knew what we needed to do. Make sure you complete a budget so you know what is going out every week and what income you need in order to survive. When I left the bank, I was making $45,000 p.a. I have got to say, I was driven a bit by money and was going to be rapt if I could make $80,000 p.a. It took me a few years to reach my goal, but I did, and there was definitely a lot of support from my family in order for me to get there.

Marketing – Try Things Outside the Square and Be Persistent

Remember, you're a walking advertisement for your business. Make sure you are presentable all the time and conduct yourself in a manner that represents your business professionally. Being outgoing is foreign to a lot of people; you just need to be yourself. If you act in a way that is not who you really are, people will see through you straight away.

You need to talk to as many people as you can – not necessarily about yourself and what you do, but you need to ask people what they do and listen. People love talking about themselves, especially if you show genuine interest in them. Try and ask them a question or relate a story back to what they are talking about. Eventually, they will return the favour and ask you what you do; if they don't, they're not worth knowing anyway. This is a way you will get your name out there; it's a way of building your brand. Networking events and social events are the best way to meet people and talk business.

You need to have a few ways to get business in the door. Make sure all your family and friends know what you are doing. Don't be scared to try different marketing ideas.

When I first started, I used to send a letter to properties that were listed on the internet. The letter had a fresh tea bag stapled to the top left hand corner of the letter and it stated that selling a property was stressful, now sit down and have a cuppa on me and if you need assistance in getting finance for your next purchase then give me a call. Did I have a great strike rate with this idea? Not really, but it was a marketing idea I was prepared to try and it didn't cost a lot. I also used to send an introduction letter to real estate agents, then follow it up with a phone call. Trust me, not a lot of your competitors will be doing these things that are different; you need to be persistent and don't give up. Sure, you might have a better strike rate with a web page or social media, but don't be afraid to try different things. There is a lot of satisfaction when you try something different and it comes off.

Get your thinking caps on.

Overview

I don't think there is one secret formula to be successful in business. You need to hit it head-on with everything you have and be prepared that there are going to be struggles and successes. It's about learning – learning about your industry, learning about yourself and learning from your mistakes. I have made plenty of mistakes, but I have been prepared to take risks.

What might work well for you may not work well for others, and that could be due to a whole host of reasons. I'm not a big one for setting goals and making business plans, but that's not to say it isn't for you. All I can suggest is to build your knowledge, know your product, surround yourself with the right people and give it a go. And if that doesn't work, give it a go again. I've made mistakes, I'll make plenty more, but I'd like to think my passion will get me through in the end.

Lastly, I was given a saying when I was younger by a massive influence in my life, my father: 'Winners make it happen; losers let it happen.'

Make Informed Choices

Tony Carmusciano

Tony owns Woodbridge Insurance Services Pty Ltd.

Owning your own business can be very rewarding if you go about it the right way.

I was born on 14 September 1958 to immigrant parents who came from Sicily post-WWII with nothing but their suitcases and terror of coming to a land spoken of as 'the land of opportunity'.

Unable to speak one word of English, they embarked on a life of creating opportunities for their future generations. To say that they, like many other immigrants of their time, struggled is an understatement. They both worked in labour-type jobs, grabbing as many hours of overtime as they could and eventually bought and paid off their first home.

That was to be the foundation for their family, an opportunity that they would never have been able to realise in their beloved Sicily. To this day, both aged in their 80s, they are proud of their achievements and grateful to a country that has afforded them the opportunity to work hard and build their wealth.

As parents, their focus was to provide us with opportunities that they did not have – education, and all the benefits that come from that. I can proudly say that my parents not only gave me that opportunity, but brought my younger sister and I up to appreciate things and to realise that to get what you want, you have to be prepared to work hard for it.

Post 'Form 6' (Year 12 to most of you), I decided that, like most of my friends, I wanted to join the workforce. I had no idea of what I wanted to do. My father wanted to buy me a ute and a toolbox and set me up as a tradesman – I was never one to want to get my hands dirty, so I decided to look for office work. There were a number of interviews, all at insurance companies (not that I had any understanding of what insurance was then), and I was lucky to be offered a job by a tired looking old man at FAI Insurance.

FAI's building was an old rabbit warren – messy and dark, but I was excited and had absolutely no idea of what my job was. The next morning, the phone rang and the agency had set up another interview. My mum insisted that I attend the interview 'just in case' (to this day I still don't understand the 'just in case' bit), but MLC's building was new, and the women in the office wore nice uniforms.

I spent most of my time in the interview looking at the women (hey, I was only 18!). I can still hear the roar in Royce Laycock's laugh when he asked me what I'd do if they offered me a job and I answered honestly that I'd accept theirs ahead of FAI as I think I could enjoy working here! Well, I got the job not just on the back of my good looks ... oops, I mean honesty.

Little did I know, that day was the

beginning of a lifetime career, embarking on a journey that taught me so much. Importantly, it has shown me the importance of protecting important things in life: family, possessions and the disastrous effect of losing one's assets and ability to earn their income.

My job at MLC started as the mail boy, looking after stationery, and doing the banking. Over the next few years I progressed to underwriting and was 'promoted' to the claims department. That's when I started really learning about insurance. You also see a different side of people, the ugly side when they realise that they are not going to get back from insurance what they expected.

This was never more evident than after the Macedon Fires in the early '80s. The company that I was working for at the time (Vanguard Insurance, later to become WMG – affectionately referred to as 'Wogs, Macedonians & Greeks!') insured most of the Australian Airways staff. That was my first experience of witnessing how under-insurance affected real people. Most, if not all, had no idea that their policies were not adequate enough to rebuild their homes. Nearly all did not have enough contents insurance. I met many of them who came into our office to collect the cheques. I recall paying out between $150,000 to $ 300,000 to each client, and in every instance, I saw people devastated at not only losing their precious and sentimental effects, but also the realisation that they simply would not get anywhere enough to rebuild their homes, let alone furnish them.

Over the years, I witnessed many cases of businesses being ruined after major incidents such as fires, storms, burglaries, etc. As saddening as it was to see the real devastation that this causes to families, I learnt that those who dealt through insurance brokers also suffered the same consequences – the effects of under insurance, or not having the right cover.

When, in 2001, I became an insurance broker, I set out on my own crusade of making sure that my clients were best protected by having adequate sums insured and having the best possible cover. Reality hit quickly. Whilst I was focused on offering commercial clients the best protection they could get, I wasn't the one paying the premiums. I had little understanding of the pressures on businesses and the need to reduce costs as much as possible. So my first lesson was to learn what it was the client needed. To do that, I not only had to understand what the business was about, but what needed to happen after a major incident such as a fire. Now that is going to be different in every case.

So that my clients didn't go bust just by paying for their insurances, I had to get an appreciation of the financial strength of the business or family that owned it, and their ability to be able to recover financially after a major loss.

Please understand that most see insurance as a necessary evil. How many businesses have Public Liability or Professional Indemnity insurance only because they have to provide customers with evidence that they have that cover?

I am still horrified today at how many small businesses do not have those two covers in place. Some stupidly think that nothing will ever happen to them. That's fine until a customer suffers a financial loss and all hell breaks loose with legal action. Sadly, it is the smaller businesses that will see owners lose everything, even their homes, which some think may be protected.

My challenge is to educate my clients about what products they ought to consider. I am passionate about putting my clients in a position so they can make an informed decision about protecting their assets and their livelihood.

Having worked as an employee over many years, I had the urge to start my own company so that I could do things 'my way'. That means allowing ample time to better understand what clients' needs really are and how major events can affect their businesses and, in turn, their livelihoods.

To do this, you need to dedicate a lot of time for each client, and as everyone in business knows, time is money. Yet my passion is to do it right and get the best protection that my clients need, so there was my first challenge – getting the right balance so that I gave each client the time that was needed, without driving myself into financial ruin by over-servicing.

This was relatively easy to fix – extend the work hours and soon enough a 45-hour week became an 80-odd-hour week, not counting the occasions I'd 'have just a quick look at my emails' and walk out of the office two hours later. Time management became a major problem, as I was determined to allocate whatever time was necessary in order to do the job that I wanted to achieve.

The time factor also led to other problems – taking the eye off the ball in important matters, such as Credit Control. Ensuring that clients paid premiums within credit terms. Insurers provide credit terms, and it is easy to renew an insurance policy, send the invoice out to clients and then expect them to pay it immediately. My outstanding debtors report eventually grew to a point that it was a major effort every week to contend with and to collect monies from clients before the insurers cancel covers due to non-payment.

Put simply, I can work as hard as I want, but until such time as clients pay their premiums, I do not earn a cent.

Most clients are quite good and will pay premiums within 14 days. It's that 15% that 'lose' or forget to pay it that you need to be on top of.

My solution to that is to look at my debtors twice weekly to ensure I know who is going to pay and when. Once any client gets to 30 days and I do not know how or when they are going to pay, it is time to take steps to sort it out – they either want the cover or not. Just find out whichever it is.

As the business grew, more and more clients were having claims. Not that I want my clients' businesses to be disrupted by having losses, but it's great when it does happen and they are satisfied with how the claim was handled and the payments received.

Claims mean time also because clients need to feel that they are given the time and service during those occasions when they most need help.

In all my years of being a broker, it's funny how every time that a client calls notifying me about a claim, I immediately think, *Geez, did I renew that policy*, or, *Did I add that car to the fleet?* Fortunately, there has never been a problem. I guess it's like driving up to a booze bus and being nervous about doing a breathalyser, even though you haven't had a drink all night!

But claims are time consuming and a challenge. The largest claim that I have been involved in took over 100 hours of my time. This is very taxing on any business, but essential service that must be provided – after all, that's what my commissions and fees are charged for.

Claims are one of my biggest marketing points. A customer who is satisfied with the outcome of a claim will always be a good one to refer business opportunities to me. So far, in the little over two years that we have been operating, I have received half a dozen referrals from this alone.

Getting back to my passion: ensuring that my clients make informed decisions to best protect themselves. This can lead to much anguish when all I hear are concerns about the cost. Never, after a major incident like a fire, have I ever heard a client talk about the cost of the insurance. The question has always been 'Do I have the cover?' or 'Do I have enough cover?'

The outcome of any claim will depend on these two questions, as well as a few other matters.

However, the cost to any business in not having either the right – or enough – cover can mean financial ruin. This almost always results in hardship and ruin where it hurts us most – the family.

I've had years of experience in this industry, as well as an inside view to other businesses, so I feel very well qualified to give some tips to anyone thinking about going out on their own.

You must have a **Business Plan**. Without one, it is very easy to get distracted and lose your way. It must be reviewed frequently and you must be prepared to modify it if the situation requires that.

The plan should be very detailed, as it demonstrates to you, as much as anyone else that you may show it to, that you are very clear in what it is you aim to achieve and how you plan to get there.

I started my business in June 2011 and I had no idea of how important this document was going to be to me. After two and a half years, I can assure anyone wanting to start up a new business that it will be very easy to lose your way. To this day, I still refer to it frequently.

An old friend of mine insisted that I spend as much time on it as possible and I put a lot of emphasis on the marketing aspect. My business started as a truly microscopic business – my concern was that the income in the first year was not going to amount to much at all. So that leads me to the second important element of any new business – capitalisation.

You must have **sufficient funds** in the business. I planned setting up my business for over a year. In that time, I saved up a pool of funds so that I could set up my business, and be able to draw a salary for six months. I always knew that I had to be patient at the outset, as in my industry the income takes a little time to filter through. I did start to stress out a little after not seeing much income hit the bank account in the first four months, but I was prepared for this and I had the funds to carry me through. I had to keep focused on and execute my business plan.

Another thing I did well was to document things. As an insurance broker, making detailed notes is an essential element of the job. As a business owner, I had no idea how important it was to document much, much more. For instance, I ran head first into trouble on the accounts by not documenting all my actions. My poor bookkeeper had no idea of what I was doing until such time as I was told in no uncertain manner that I had to start putting pen to paper and making notes 'for others to follow'. Funny thing is that people who look at my client files compliment me on how well they are documented. Sadly, I struggled on the admin side. I have had to master that aspect of being a business owner!

Owning and operating my own business has brought me much pleasure, not to mention the rewards of having some success. I strongly encourage anyone to consider starting their own business. It's hard work, with many a sleepless night, and you must be prepared to work very long hours, especially at the outset. However, the reward is something that you will cherish for a long time to come.

Each milestone is a special memory, be it winning that first client off your own bat or the first time that someone refers someone to you, but the most memorable moment (for me) was the first cheque that arrived in the mail – it was mine!

Take Action

Phil Schibeci

Professional speaker, workshop facilitator, mentor, coach and author, Phil helps people be the best they can be.

I was born into an Italian Roman Catholic family as Felice Salvatore Roberto Schibeci – although my friends just call me Phil! – and grew up behind a fruit shop on Lygon Street in Carlton, an inner suburb of Melbourne. Lygon Street wasn't full of restaurants and night-life in those days as it is now. In fact I'd ride my tricycle up and down the footpath on weekdays after all the shops closed at 5.00pm.

My parents were hard-working Italian immigrants and they did what many Italian immigrants of that time did: bought a fruit shop business and used the proceeds from the business to purchase residential investment properties. So business and investment had an early influence on my life.

At this young age I religiously went to church every Sunday. I didn't really know why I did this; it just seemed a good idea. One particular Sunday when I was eight-years-old listening to the priest deliver a powerful sermon, I decided that when I grew up, speaking to groups of people for a living would be a lot more fun than working in an office doing a boring job.

At the same age, I also successfully entertained my classmates while up on stage – I even made the teacher laugh, and she was a nun! This further fuelled my desire to want to speak to people rather than get a regular job like everyone else.

These two events were to have a profound impact on my life.

Despite my upbringing it wasn't until I was in my forties that I finally started my own business, and it's taken a lot of courage and determination to get to where I am today.

These days I help business owners and individuals discover what they really want and how to create a powerful purpose so they can live each day with passion and achieve their full potential. I show people how to overcome their fears and challenge them to take massive action on their big ideas and dreams.

Over the years I have participated extensively in world-class personal and professional development programs. During the last twenty-one years I have taught and facilitated public speaking, presentation, communication and leadership skills to people from all walks of life. I use a variety of methods that I customise for each person and group I work with.

After working with me people are equipped with life-changing skills that enable them to be more effective in their personal and professional lives. Despite all of this I consider my biggest achievement to be my thirty-two-year marriage to Mary, and raising two daughters who, as adults, still love to talk to their dad!

I Decide to Make My Dream a Reality

It was a forgettable Monday morning at work. While reflecting on my life and feeling very unhappy and sorry for myself, I had a life-defining moment.

I remembered how about fifteen years earlier, I had set myself some very big goals to make a difference in the world. Achieving those goals was going to make me, and others, very happy and I was going to earn a lot of money doing so.

But that day it suddenly hit me; here I was in this job doing what I had been doing for the last 25 years, while dreaming about doing something else.

I felt like I had wasted years of my life going in circles while fooling myself that I was heading towards my goals, but in reality getting nowhere.

This realisation was initially depressing, but eventually it would also prove to be very liberating. It reminded me of a saying I once heard: 'The truth shall set you free, but first it will piss you off.'

At that time I was definitely at the 'pissed off' stage. For about fifteen years I had gone from one job to another feeling like I was doing something about making a change. The reality was that I didn't like what I was doing and I didn't have clear goals or a plan of how to get what I wanted.

Although for many years I had been doing what I was passionate about outside of my normal working hours, my dream was to run my own business doing what I loved – that is, helping others achieve their goals and dreams. I was in my forties and was no closer to my goal than when I first created it all those years ago.

What was worse, I couldn't see how I was going to achieve any of the things I really wanted. That horrible Monday morning at work after my boss had berated me over an insignificant mistake was my life-defining moment. For the first time in my life I had the horrible thought that I might not actually achieve what I wanted in this lifetime.

The fear of not achieving my dreams became my motivation to finally develop a plan detailing step-by-step how I was going to get from where I was to where I wanted to be. Part of the plan included the timeframe in which I was going to achieve my goals. I started also to become aware of all the different voices in my head telling me what I could and couldn't do and I realised that the little eight-year-old was still there in the background struggling to get my attention. As soon as I pushed all the negative voices aside I could hear him. There he was. After all these years he hadn't given up on me. As I got closer to him I could hear what he was saying: 'Phil, come on, follow your dreams. You can do it; it'll be lots of fun!'

I think we all have a child within us and we just need to occasionally stop and listen to the important message that's there waiting for us.

For years I went in circles jumping from one idea to another, and when I did take action I expected immediate results, all the while without any specific plan in place to give me direction. It would seem like a good idea rather than something I desperately wanted. I wasn't willing to push through all the hard stuff that was holding me back. I've now learnt that this is necessary for success – if it was easy everyone would be doing it.

I've heard it said that we overestimate what we can achieve in twelve months and underestimate what we can achieve in five years. I was definitely doing this. A lack of a plan and consistent action was causing me to get very frustrated and disheartened.

As long as we keep striving towards our goals, we are not failures. It's when we give up on what we desire that we can be considered a failure. Sometimes I have felt like giving up because things don't seem to be going my way, but fortunately for me, no matter how difficult things seem to get, I just keep moving forward.

A Call to Action

What was missing for me for a long time and what might be missing for you is a lack of action. I spent a lot of time thinking about what I wanted to do with my life, but besides some occasional bursts (or outbursts) of action, I didn't do much about it consistently.

Not being accustomed to actually following up my goals with action is probably why some things I did, looking back now, were really silly. I won't go into the details. Suffice to say I surprised myself at how bold I could be at times. But I learnt from my mistakes and kept moving forward by taking more and more ongoing, consistent and positive actions.

These days taking massive action has become more of a habit for me and I don't have to think about doing it as much as

I used to. As long as I continue building momentum my confidence and self-belief grows. As soon as I stop or hesitate I've noticed how easy apathy and inaction quickly set in. What I've learnt is that the more actions I take the quicker my plans unfold and become real.

Who would have known that for things to happen you have to actually do something?

The huge insight I got from this time in my life was that I had just expected things to happen. Working in a job that I disliked with people I didn't have much in common with (other than the fact that most of us didn't seem to enjoy our jobs) drove this home to me in a very confronting way. It was at that time that I finally realised that for my goals to actually happen I was going to have to make some big changes.

I started taking lots of action doing anything that I thought would take me in the direction I wanted to go. During the next twelve months not much seemed to change. Then suddenly everything started to fall into place and my life started what was to become an extraordinary transformation. Everything – and I mean everything – started to go right for me. My relationships, my career, my finances and my health all started to head in the right direction. Then something interesting happened: I became scared of my life becoming bigger than what I thought I could handle. Fortunately I didn't let this fear stop me and I kept taking the next step, one after the other. After a while I started to get excited about it becoming bigger than me. In fact this is exactly what I wanted, for my life to become huge! I found that instead of this fear being the thing that stopped me it was now what motivated me to keep going. And keep going I did!

People were now inviting me to come and speak at their meetings as a guest speaker. After one of my presentations, a friend came up to me and said that he found it inspiring to see me grow and improve so much over such a short period of time. I was on my way to achieving everything I had always wanted and I couldn't turn back even if I wanted to. The positive energy I was now radiating was causing me to attract lots of other positive people into my life.

I've lived most of my adult life unhappy and unfulfilled and one of the biggest thrills I get now is when people comment on how happy I am. The reason I like hearing this is because it reminds me of how much I'm enjoying my life now and how far I've come with my change in attitude and outlook. It also reminds me that I'm no longer in a rut.

I never thought that I could love my life as much as I do now, and the best part about it is that it continues to get better every single day.

I've continued to live my life using the principles and techniques I've written about in my book, which I know work for both others and myself. As a result I'm now much happier and fulfilled, which has resulted in improved relationships, a great lifestyle and a much clearer understanding of others and myself.

I face more challenges now on a daily basis than I could ever have imagined. Often I'm feeling scared and uncomfortable because I'm doing things that are outside my comfort zone and yet I'm having a lot more fun. I'm also more satisfied and content helping others and my life just keeps getting better and better.

Make Sure You Have a Plan That Works for You

Once I made the decision that my life was going to change I needed a plan to make it happen. I knew the first thing that would occur when I started my business was that I would be taking a significant pay cut. As a result of this amazing foresight I decided to take the advice of the author of *Rich Dad Poor Dad*, Robert Kiyosaki. In his book he suggests that when you initially start a new business don't give up your day job. So I decided I would gradually reduce the hours I put in at my day job and increase the amount of time and effort I put into growing my business.

I started by quitting full-time employment and got a contract position that allowed me to work just three days a week. Soon I started doing the same work from home, which gave me even more flexibility while I slowly built my business income. At the same time I did a joint venture property development using the knowledge I had built up over the years about property investing. With the proceeds from the sale of the properties safely tucked away in the bank I had a financial and emotional safety buffer to any possible cash flow issues. This allowed me to stop my now part-time job and focus solely on my new business. The interesting thing is that money has pretty much gone untouched, which enables me to now invest it in the share market and earn some passive income.

Over the last 21 years I have invested heavily in my financial, professional and personal education. All of this knowledge and learning comes in handy when you go out on your own.

I would like to make a very important point here regarding success. With all the things I've done, am doing now and will do in the future I have one golden rule: *they must be activities that I enjoy.* Take the property and share investing for example; yes I do them to generate income, but I choose to participate in a manner in which I enjoy doing them. From my experience and observations of others, too many people fail to make their major life goals a reality because they try to achieve them by focusing on too many activities they don't enjoy. They consume a lot of time and energy convincing themselves that they need to do these things they don't like doing in order to get what they want. The end result is they burn out, end up frustrated and in a rut and give up just before reaching their big goal. Please, no matter what advice you get or what anyone tells you, don't fall into this trap! You must enjoy the journey, otherwise you won't last the distance.

Enthusiasm: The Secret to Remaining Young and Healthy

One thing I've noticed that's different about me compared to most people my age is my enthusiasm, curiosity and willingness to learn new things, which often involves doing something that initially may feel uncomfortable.

At my 50th birthday party my two daughters did a slideshow presentation about me. One of their slides stated that my enthusiasm for life was an inspiration.

As a parent I usually only hear things like, 'Dad, you're so lame', because I do things like take photos of sunsets and sunrises. So to hear both of my daughters say that my enthusiasm for life was an inspiration was very moving. I believe that this attitude will keep a person young. Many people my age act like their life is almost over. I, on the other hand, like a little kid am still very enthusiastic and inquisitive, wanting to learn and do new things. I'm now in my fifties and I'm still working out what I'm going to do with my life when I grow up!

If you want to remain young, both physically and mentally, always maintain a ferocious curiosity and enthusiasm for life.

Make the Journey

Sometimes it's not so much about the destination as it is about the journey, and as I mentioned earlier you must enjoy the journey if you want to reach your destination.

I've been on my journey for as long as I care to remember and I still don't feel I'm anywhere near arriving at my destination. I'm starting to think that I may not ever feel that I have arrived, and that's probably a good thing. You see, one of the things I've realised is that, if life isn't a bold adventure, then what's the point of it all?

Recent surveys of older people, and especially those who have passed the hundred-year mark, asked them what they would have done differently if they could live their lives over again. Most of them said that they would have taken more risks and tried more things. They would have ventured into new jobs, activities, and relationships. They also said that other people's decisions and demands largely shaped their lives. Don't let this happen to you!

If you want things to change, you need to change things. The more you do what you are doing, the more you'll get what you've got.

Now that I've started to live a life I love I will keep setting myself challenging goals for the rest of my life and I will strive to achieve them. But when I'm finished with this life it won't be what I've achieved that will be most important. I think the most important thing will be that I attempted to do things that, at first, I thought were beyond me, and also it will be about the people I met and learnt from and the ones that I made a difference to along the way.

Use what you think will be useful to you on your journey from what you learn from others and discard the rest. Also, make sure you enjoy the journey and make a difference to as many people as you possibly can along the way.

My Final Challenge to You

A number of years ago I went to visit my uncle who was in an old peoples' home. My uncle was a wealthy man. He owned many properties and lived in a big house on his own by the sea. His wife had passed away a number of years before and now he could no longer look after himself and had to be cared for by others. That day I realised that no matter what we achieve in our lives, no matter how much wealth and possessions we acquire we will all end up in a situation similar to my uncle's. This was both depressing and motivating. That day I realised how important it was to live a life focused on doing what I am passionate about rather than playing it safe and trying to build security.

Determine the steps you need to take, especially the first step, and then, as Brian Tracy states in his book, *Reinvention*, 'Have the courage and conviction to step out in faith in the direction of your dreams. The willingness and the courage to take the first step is often the turning point in our lives.'

When I made the whole class and nun laugh on that school stage when I was 8, I experienced a strong feeling of hope and optimism. Anything was possible. With great effort and determination I have managed to recapture those feelings as an adult by doing what I enjoy. I'm very good at what I do and therefore get paid well, but the best thing is that it feels wonderful. If I can do this at a mature age, so can YOU!

Thus, here's my challenge to you …

- if your mind is stuck in a rut;

- if you don't think you can get out of the Monday to Friday, 9 to 5 grind;

- if you don't spend enough time with your family or doing the things you love;

- if you feel stressed, unhappy, dissatisfied and constantly under pressure;

- if you don't think you are capable of doing what you want with your life;

… then go to an old people's home and see what is in store for you. If that doesn't give you the courage to take charge of your life nothing will.

If you are not living the life you dream of when you are young and healthy you are not going to do it when you are old and frail. You have an opportunity NOW to change your future.

Move into action.

Grab hold of your life.

It's yours for the taking!

Self-Made Call to Action

Justin Fankhauser: Every day, in business and in life, I come across things that scare me, but the thing I always do is have a go and never give up. Most people in business and in life always take the easy option. I always have a go. Even if it doesn't work out, **have a crack.**

Jamie Thomas: If budget and time allows (note: make time) enrol in a short business course before venturing out alone so that you understand those key business principles. Understand the value in investing in education and continuous learning. A short business course laid the foundation for a basic understanding of running a business. Training prepared me for the challenge. **Invest in yourself**, because it's an investment in your future.

Melissa Baker: Education is an ongoing lesson. As my husband says quite regularly, 'Every day is a school day'. It's one of the most important investments we can make in our businesses; I don't think we can ever stop learning. Don't be scared of making mistakes either. Most importantly, learn from them. **Learn from your mistakes**. It's the best teacher life will give you.

Steven Briffa: I had gone through life without a plan. Instead of giving up on my dream, though, I decided to change my plans. More importantly, I decided to change my mindset. When another setback hit, I looked at the situation again but from a different angle. The Chinese word for 'crisis' is composed of two characters that represent 'danger' and 'opportunity'. This was my opportunity. **Recognise and seize your opportunity**.

Blaise van Hecke: Owning a business is creating a lifestyle for yourself. It can be hard work and it can be frustrating, but if you set up your structures and systems it will get easier as your name becomes known. In our business, we come up with an idea, get excited and say, 'What a fantastic idea! Let's work out how to make it happen.' Every business has its own story. Make sure you **engage people with your story**.

Paul Blake: Create a synergy group, a group of experts you can draw on if your clients need those services. I brought into my group an accountant, conveyancer, real estate agent, financial planner, leasing consultant and insurance broker. If you have a client who needs any of these services, you can refer them. Similarly, those in your group can refer you. Make sure you **create good synergies**.

Tony Carmusciano: My challenge is to educate my clients about what products they ought to consider. I am passionate about putting my clients in a position so they can make an informed decision about protecting their assets and their livelihood. **Make informed decisions**.

Phil Schibeci: If you're stuck in a rut, if you don't think you can get out of the 9 to 5 grind, if you don't spend enough time with your family or doing the things you love, if you feel stressed, unhappy, dissatisfied, if you don't think you are capable of doing what you want with your life, then go to an old people's home and see what is in store for you. You have an opportunity NOW to change your future. **Take action** to live the life you want!

Biographies

You've read their stories and gotten to know them, but here's how to find out more about our *Self-Made* authors, as well as their businesses.

Melissa Baker, is the director of Enrichment Property Group, as well as a director of Enrichment's sister business, Mel Baker Property Management.

Phone: 0416 242 876
Email: mel@melbaker.com.au
Web: melbaker.com.au

Paul Blake is a mortgage broker with the boutique finance broking company Citiwide Homeloans.

Citiwide Homeloans
Suite 1, 204–218 Dryburgh St
North Melbourne, Victoria 3051

Phone: 1300 345 747
Mobile: 0407 345572
Email: paul@citiwide.com.au
Web: citiwide.com.au / paulblake
Facebook: Citiwide Homeloans Northcote
Linked In: Paul Blake

Steven Briffa is the Owner/Strategic Director of Plenty Valley Printing.

Plenty Valley Printing
165 Para Road
Greensborough, Victoria 3088

Telephone: 03 9432 1955
Mobile: 0411 472 669
Email: Steve@pvprinting.com.au
Web: pvprinting.com.au

Tony Carmusciano is the owner of Woodbridge Insurance Services.

Woodridge Insurance Services P/L
PO Box 182
Eltham, Victoria 3095

Mobile: 0488 992 445
Telephone: (03) 9852 4910

Authorised Representative No. 407101
ABN No. 28151495822

Justin Fankhauser is a co-founder and owner/manager of TopLock Locksmiths.

TopLock Locksmiths
22/148 Arthurton Road
Northcote, Victoria 3070

Phone: 1300 679 979
Email: justin@toploplock.net.au
Web: www.toplock.net.au
Facebook: http://www.facebook.com/ToplockLocksmiths
Twitter: http://twitter.com/#!/toplock24x7
YouTube: http://www.youtube.com/user/toplock23?feature=results_main
LinkedIn: http://www.linkedin.com/company/toplock-locksmiths

Phil Schibeci is a professional speaker, workshop facilitator, mentor, coach and author of *How to Get Out of The RUT Race*, a practical guide to provide readers the tools to get out of a rut and achieve major life goals.

Phone: 0409 848 840
Web: philschibeci.com
Email: phil@therutrace.com
Linkedin: Phil Schibeci
Facebook: https://www.facebook.com/
phil.schibeci
Twitter: https://twitter.com/PhilSchibeci

Jamie Thomas is the Brand and Marketing Specialist at Synkd, a marketing and design company.

Synkd
Level 10
50 Market Street
Melbourne, Victoria 3000

Phone: 1300 748 823
Email: mail@synkd.com.au
Web: synkd.com.au
LinkedIn: au.linkedin.com/in/
jamiethomasau
Facebook: facebook/synkddesign
Pinterest: pinterest.com/synkd

Blaise van Hecke is author of *The Book Book: 12 Steps to Successful Publishing* and co-founder and publisher at Busybird Publishing.

Busybird Publishing
2/118 Para Road
Montmorency, Victoria 3094

Phone: (03) 9434 6365
Email: busybird@bigpond.net.au
Web: busybird.com.au
Facebook: Busybird-Publishing
Twitter: https://twitter.com/busybusybird
LinkedIn: Blaise van Hecke